JAKE'S JOKES
A RADICAL JOKE BOOK

PUFFIN BOOKS

UK | USA | Canada | Ireland | Australia
India | New Zealand | South Africa

Puffin Books is part of the Penguin Random House group of companies whose addresses can be found a
global.penguinrandomhouse.com.

puffinbooks.com

This edition first published 2016
Content first published 2015
001

The National Literacy Trust is a registered charity no: 1116260 and a company limited by guarantee no. 58
registered in England and Wales and a registered charity in Scotland no. SC042944. Registered address: 68
Lambeth Road, London SW8 1RL.
National Literacy Trust logo and reading tips © National Literacy Trust 2016
www.literacytrust.org.uk/donate

Set in Pendlefont
Printed in Great Britain

A CIP catalogue record for this book is available from the British Library

ISBN: 978-0-141-37073-6

www.greenpenguin.co.uk

PUFFIN

What did Finn's hat say to the rest of Finn's clothes?
You stay here, I'll go on a head.

What kind of mathematics does the Cosmic Owl like?
Owl-gebra!

Jake: Knock, knock!
Ice King: Who's there?
Jake: Ivor.
Ice King: Ivor who?
Jake: Ivor you let us in, Ice King, or we're climbing through the window!

4

Jake: Bro, I was surrounded by lions this morning.
Finn: Really? Lions?

Jake: Yeah. Dandelions! HAHAHA.

What is the Never Ending Pie Throwing Robot's favourite planet?
Neptr-tune!

Jake: I'm going to stand outside the Tree Fort.
So, if anyone asks, I'm outstanding!

What does Jake say when he exits the Tree Fort?
I'm leaf-ing!

What does Finn find easy to get into but hard to get out of?
Trouble!

What do you call Tree Trunks when she doesn't matter?
Irr-elephant!

What's better than adventuring?
NOTHING.

What does Finn say when BMO doesn't want to play games?
BMO-re fun!

What's yellow on the inside and green on the outside?
Banana Man dressed up as a cucumber.

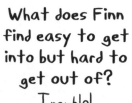

Why does the Tree Fort hate maths?
Because it doesn't want square roots.

How does the ocean say hello?
It waves.

Finn: I bet I can make you say purple.
Jake: How?
Finn: What colour is Princess Bubblegum?
Jake: Pink.
Finn: I told you I could make you say pink!
Jake: What the huh?! You said purple!
Finn: Ha! Dude, I told you I could make you say purple!

This joke is less funny if you have thalassophobia.

Why is six scared
of seven?
Because seven eight nine!

When is a door
not a door?
When it's a jar.

What's brown
and sticky?
A stick.

What has a bed
you can't sleep in?
A river!

What do you call a fly with
no wings?
A walk.

Why did the snail go to the Tree Fort?
We don't know. He still hasn't got there!

What would you call it if
Shelby took over the world?
Global worming.

What kind of room in the Tree
Fort can you not go inside?
A mushroom.

Why does Finn make other
people want to be heroes?
Because he's Finn-spirational!

What do you call
a cow that eats
grass?
A lawn-mooer!

What should an adventurer
take on a trip to the desert?
A thirst aid kit!

Why did the squirrel run
round and round in circles?
He'd gone a little nuts.

Why did the monster start
eating candles?
For some light refreshment!

On which days do monsters
like to eat heroes?
Chewsday.

What kind of weapon
grows on the ground?
A blade of grass!

What did BMO say
when he overcharged
his batteries?

I'M IN SHOCK!

What did the
beaver say to
the Tree Fort?
It's been nice
gnawing you.

What did the
Tree Fort say
when all its
leaves fell off?
I don't be-leaf it!

Why did the Tree Fort
go to the doctor?
Because it had a
window pane.

What's BMO's favourite kind of snack?
Computer chips!

What does the Tree Fort have in common with an elephant?
They both have trunks.

What's the best thing to put in an apple pie baked by Tree Trunks?
Your teeth!

Finn: Knock, knock!
Jake: Who's there?
Finn: Orange.
Jake: Orange who?
Finn: Orange you going to let me in, man?!

What kind of rocks are never found in the ocean?
Dry ones.

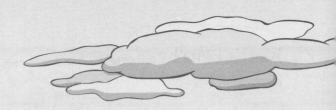

How does the Tree Witch get around?
She witch-hikes!

What do you call a man in a hole?
Doug!

What do you call a man overlooking the ocean?
Cliff!

Why does Banana Man wear suntan lotion? Because otherwise he'd peel!

How do you catch a squirrel? Climb a tree and act like a nut!

How do you send a message in the forest? By moss code.

What does Finn call the end of a heroic battle? The Finnale!

If you drop your sword in the mud, what will you get out? A dirty sword. Duh.

Jake: Knock, knock!
Finn: Who's there?
Jake: Bark!
Finn: Bark who?
Jake: I'm barking because I'm a dog.

What do you call Jake when he gets angry? Barking mad!

What's the most lethal part of any joke? The punchline.

What do you do when life gives you lemons? Do NOT make a Lemongrab!

Why did Finn throw food on Jake?
Because Jake said, "Dinner is on me!"

What do you call the Snail without his shell?
Homeless!

Finn: Knock, knock!
Jake: Who's there?
Finn: Boo!
Jake: Boo who?
Finn: Hey, man, don't cry! It's only me!

What drink would a hero give an evil monster?
Fruit PUNCH!

# Marceline's Creepy Bonus Jokes

What's red, red and red all over?
Don't know but it sounds delicious!

What do you call a vampire
who's totally lost it?
Batty!

Why don't skeletons
fight each other?
Because they don't
have the guts!

Why can't skeletons
play music?
Because they
don't have organs.

What do you call two witches who live together?
Broom-mates.

What soup do vampires eat?
Alpha-BAT soup.

Why did I throw the clock out of the window?
To see time fly like me!

What kind of letters do famous vampires get?
Fang mail!

What's a vampire's favourite fruit?
Neck-tarines!

What happened to the Ice King when all the princesses escaped?
He had a meltdown!

What did the Ice King say before beginning his comedy routine?
This is gonna sleigh you!

Why doesn't the Ice King need to sleep much?
Because he's always kid-napping!

Why is Ice King so sad?
He feels ice-olated!

What do you call Gunter when it's in the Fire Kingdom?
Lost!

What do you get when you cross Marceline and Snow Golem?
Frostbite.

What's black and white and black and white and black and white?
Gunter rolling down a mountain.

What's the biggest problem with snow boots?
They melt!

22

What's black and white and pink and black and white and pink?
Gunthalina rolling down a mountain.

What's black and white and red all over?
Gunter with a sunburn.

Why do princesses not want to marry the Ice King?
Because he treats them so coldly!

What do you call an ice palace in a heatwave?
A puddle!

What was the Ice King's favourite part of school?
Snow and tell!

Finn: Knock, knock!
Ice King: Who's there?
Finn: Harry.
Ice King: Harry who?
Finn: Harry up and let us in, it's freezing out here!

What do the Snow Men call their offspring?
Chilly-dren.

How does Snow Golem get to work?
By icicle!

How do you keep from getting cold feet in the Ice Kingdom?
Don't go brrrr-footed!

What did Ice King say to the escaping princess?
Freeze!

Ice King: Knock, knock!
Princess Bubblegum: Who's there?
Ice King: Olive!
Princess Bubblegum: Olive who?
Ice King: Olive you, Princess!
JUST MARRY ME, ALREADY!

Why doesn't the Ice Palace get cold in the winter?
Because it wears a snowcap!

Why is Ricardio the Heart Guy great at playing music?
Because he always has a good beat!

What's black and white and goes round and round?
Gunter in a revolving door.

What do the penguins make their beds with?
Sheets of ice and blankets of snow!

What do you get if you cross
Ice King with his drum kit?
Cool music!

What does the Ice King say
to his kidnapped princesses?
Have an ice day!

Why did the Ice King put
his money in the freezer?
He wanted cold hard cash!

What do you call it when
Kitten helps Gunter take
over the Land of Ooo?
A cat-astrophe!

What do you call a rabbit dressed up as a cake? A cream bun!

How does Princess Bubblegum freshen her breath in the lab? With experi-mints!

What kind of candy has no teeth? A gummy bear!

Why did the Banana Guard go to the doctor? Because he wasn't peeling well.

Why did Mr Cupcake
go to the Ice Kingdom?
To top up his frost-ing!

Finn: Knock, knock!
Jake: Who's there?
Finn: Doughnut.
Jake: Doughnut who?
Finn: Doughnut ask, bro . . .
it's a SECRET.

Where does Peppermint
Butler keep his photos?
On his mint-lepiece.

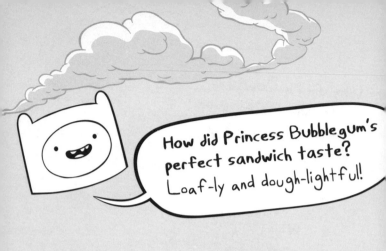

How did Princess Bubblegum's perfect sandwich taste? Loaf-ly and dough-lightful!

Why is a Candy Person's hair so sticky? Because they use a honeycomb.

Why are Candy People so popular? Because they're real sweeties!

Why did Cinnamon Bun stop looking at his body? He'd had it with the hole thing!

Why did the Gingerbread Man go to the doctor?
Because he was feeling crumby.

What do you give the Earl of Lemongrab when he's ill?
Lemon-aid.

What kind of street do Candy Zombies like best?
A dead end!

What is Science the rat's favourite game?
Hide and squeak!

How often does Princess Bubblegum look at her table of elements? Periodically!

Where do Candy People learn to make desserts? In sundae school!

Why did Lemongrab like Lemongrab 2 so much? Because he found him a-peeling!

What's rainbow-coloured and flies really fast? Lady Rainicorn, when she's in a rush!

What did Mr Cupcake say
when he got squashed?
Crumbs!

What did the fillings in PB's perfect
sandwich say to each other?
Lettuce get together!

What wobbles
as it flies?
A jelly-copter!

What
do you
call elderly
Jelly Bean
People?
Has-beans!

Why was Chocoberry
the strawberry sad?
Because her mother was in a jam!

What do you call it when
you're trapped in the
Cotton Candy Forest?
A sticky situation!

Why did Finn mess with Princess
Bubblegum's chemistry experiment?
To see if he could get a reaction!

Why are the Marshmallow Kids
always kind to everyone?
Because they're such softies.

What do you call an attractive Flame Person?
Lava-ble!

Which legend of the Fire Kingdom really likes maths?
Fire Count!

Why didn't things work out between Finn and Flame Princess?
He was too cool for her!

What kind of balls does Flame Princess like to attend?
Fireballs!

Why is Flame King a terrible chef?
He burns EVERYTHING.

What happened to
Flame Princess and
Finn's spark?
He blew it.

Who invented fire?
Some bright spark.

Which is faster: heat or cold?
Heat, because you can catch a cold!

What happens when
you cross a Flame
Person with dynamite?

An explosion!

Why is everyone in the Fire Kingdom so angry all the time?
Because they're so hot-headed!

Why else are the Flame People so angry?
Because their blood is always boiling!

Did you hear about the fire at the circus?
The heat was in tents!

What do you call it when Flame Princess attacks the Ice King's palace?
A meltdown!

How do you make fire
with two sticks?
Make sure one is a match!

What only
starts to work
after it's fired?
A rocket!

What did the
Lava Man say to
the Lava Woman?
I lava you.

What do you call
Jalapeño Pepper when
he's being nosy?
Jalapeño business!

How would Flame Princess describe
her magical scented candles?
Scent-sational!

What's the quickest way to make a Flame Guard mad at you?
Call him a candelabra.

What do you call an extra tall, extra mean-looking Flame Guard?
Sir!

Why can't you ever have ice cream in the Fire Kingdom?
Because it will melt. DUH.

What kind of food does Jalapeño Pepper like to cook?
Anything flame-grilled.

What's worse than being chased by a pack of wolves?

Being chased by a pack of Fire Wolves.

What does a Lava Man call his mother?

Mag-Ma!

What do you call a Snow Golem who makes friends with a Fire Wolf?

Water!

What's another name for the Fire Kingdom throne?

The hot seat.

What was Flame Princess and Finn's favourite song when they were a couple? Burnin' Love!

What happens when a Flame Person gets embarrassed? They feel ash-amed.

What's the best way to pet a Fire Wolf? NEVER PET A FIRE WOLF.

Unless you're happy to say goodbye to your hands.

What two seasons are there in the Fire Kingdom? Hot . . . and Hotter!

42

What does Jalapeño Pepper do when he's angry?
He gets jalapeño face!

What's hotter than the surface of the sun?
Flame Princess's temper. Ouch.

Why did the dragon breathe fire?
Because he swallowed the Flame King!

What comes out of taps in the Fire Kingdom?
Steam!

What happened when
Flame King ran really far?
He felt burned out.

What do you get if you cross Flame
Princess with a glass of water?
Steaming rage!

What does a
Lava Man wash
himself with?
Molten lather.

44

What's the least scary way to describe a volcano?
Call it a mountain with hiccups.

What kind of temper does Flame Princess have?
A fiery one!

How do the Flame People stay cool?
THEY DON'T.

What happens when a Flame Person falls in love?
Sparks fly!

# Marceline's Creepy Bonus Jokes

Why did the Skeleton Guard go to the Science Barbecue?
To get a spare rib!

What's my favourite way to get in touch with people?
To f-axe them!

How does a vampire describe something awesome?
Fang-tastic.

Why do ghosts make good cheerleaders?
Because they have a lot of spirit!

What's a monster's favourite fruit?
Boo-berries!

How do monsters like their eggs?
Terror-fried.

What do you call it when I play bass so good that a building collapses?
An axe-ident.

What do ghosts eat for dinner?
Spook-etti!

What's a mummy's favourite kind of music?
Rap!

How do you organize a Lumpy Space party?
You planet!

What's smooth and round in Lumpy Space?
LOSERS.

Why does Lumpy Space Princess look down on Brad?
Because she's SO OVER him.

What's it like travelling through a frog's mouth into Lumpy Space?
Toad-ally crazy!

LSP: Knock, knock!
Finn: Who's there?

LSP: Celeste.
Finn: Celeste who?

LSP: Celeste time I'm going to tell you a knock-knock joke.

Why did the Lumpy Space Person want to leave the party?
The atmosphere wasn't right.

What do LSP and gone-off milk have in common?
They're both spoiled and lumpy!

Finn: Hey, LSP, tell me a joke!
LSP: YOUR FACE IS A JOKE.

49

Why was Glasses feeling embarrassed?
He made a spectacle of himself.

LSP: Hey, Finn.
What kind of bomb
is the best kind?
Finn: Ummm . . . no kind?
LSP: A DRAMA BOMB!

What's the best way for
a Lumpy Space guy to
impress a regular girl?
By being smooth!

Why is Lumpy Space so cool?
Because it's totally out of this world!

Brad: Hey, LSP, do you know why you need a stepladder?
LSP: No. Why?
Brad: TO GET OVER ME.

What does LSP think is cooler than Promcoming? NOTHING. Duh.

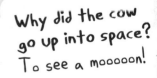

Why did the cow go up into space? To see a mooooon!

What do you call a Lumpy Space King with three eyes? A Lumpy Space Kiiing.

How is mashed potato served in Lumpy Space? With plenty of LUMPS.

When is the moon at its heaviest? When it's full.

Why didn't Finn and Jake fit in at Promcoming? Their moves were too smooth.

What does LSP eat with stew? Lumplings!

What do you call the Party
God when he goes missing?
A where-wolf!

What did one raindrop say to its
two raindrop friends?
Two's company, but three's a cloud.

What do you call a cloud that's
too lazy to stay in the sky?
Fog!

Finn: I tried to catch
some fog earlier.
Jake: Yeah? What
happened?
Finn: I mist!

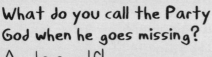

Why are Cloud People like a soggy school?
Because they're Water Elementals!

What does a rain cloud wear under its raincoat?
Thunderwear.

What did one lightning bolt say to the other?
You're shocking.

What did the evaporating raindrop say?
I'm just letting off some steam!

What is a Cloud Person when they're in the Fire Kingdom?
In trouble!

What day of the week is the least cloudy?
Sunday.

What does the Party God
do when he's amused?
He howls with laughter.

Why should you be careful
when it rains cats and dogs?
You might step in a poodle.

Why did Jake get distracted
from saving his buddy Finn?
His vision was clouded!

What kind of bow
can't be tied?
A rainbow!

What did the guy raindrop
say to the girl raindrop?
I'm really falling for you!

What did the dirt say to the rain?
Stop it or my name will be mud!

What did the straight-faced
cloud say to the joker cloud?
Are you being cirrus?!

What's a
Cloud Person's
favourite game?
Twister.

58

What is the richest
kind of air?
A million-air.

What do you call it when
two hurricanes fall in love?
A whirlwind romance.

What did the cloud say when
he was a bit confused?
I'm sorry, my mind is a little foggy!

Where is better
to party than the
Cloud Kingdom?
NOWHERE, BRO!

# Finn and Jake's Best

What kind of table has no legs?
A multiplication table.

What is Tree Trunks' favourite mathematical dessert?
Apple Pi!

What would you call a world without decimals?
Pointless!

If you had eight apples in one hand and ten in the other, what would you have?
Really big hands!

# Mathematical Jokes!

What did zero say to eight?
Nice belt!

What do you get if you divide the circumference of a pumpkin by its diameter?
Pumpkin Pi!

What shape is like a lost parrot?
A poly-gon!

Why did Finn eat his maths homework?
Because the teacher said it was a piece of cake.

Why are decimals so good at arguing?
Because they have a point!

How do you make seven even?
Take away the 's'.

Which snakes are good at sums?
Adders!

Why did the two fours skip lunch?
They already eight.

Why was the maths book sad?
Because it had too many problems!

What tool can you use when doing maths?
Multi-pliers.

What sound does a mathematical clock make?
Arithma-ticks!

How do you make one vanish?
Add a 'g' and it's gone!

What is the most mathematical season?
Sum-mer!

## Reading Tips

The **National Literacy Trust** is a charity that transforms lives through literacy. We want to get more families reading. Reading is fun and children who read in their own time do better at school and later in life. By partnering with McDonald's, we hope to encourage more families to read together.

Here are some of our top tips for reading with children.

A good way to bring a book to life is to put on different voices for different characters in the story.

Why not stop at certain points in the story to ask your child what *they* think will happen next?

Setting aside some time to read with your child every day is something both of you can look forward to.

A shared love of reading can last a lifetime. You can still read aloud to your child, even when they are confident enough to read by themselves.

If your child is excited by the subject of a story, it will help keep their interest as you read together, so help them choose the books you'll read together.